HOW ANIMALS ADAPT TO SURVIVE

FIGHTING with FANGS and CLAWS

STEPHANIE CARGILL-GREER

PowerKiDS press
New York

Published in 2018 by The Rosen Publishing Group, Inc.
29 East 21st Street, New York, NY 10010

First Edition

Editor: Elizabeth Krajnik
Book Design: Reann Nye

Photo Credits: Cover, p. 1 David W. Hamilton/Stockbyte/Getty Images; p. 5 (Gaboon viper) Shutterstock.com; p. 5 (clouded leopard) Joel Sartore/National Geographic/Getty Images; p. 5 (giant armadillo) Paul Crum/Science Source/Getty Images; p. 5 (*Therizinosaurus* claw) https://commons.wikimedia.org/wiki/File:Therizinosaurus_clawcast_aus.jpg; p. 6 Rich Carey/Shutterstock.com; p. 7 reptiles4all/Shutterstock.com; p. 9 Peter Waters/Shutterstock.com; p. 10 Vladimir Wrangel/Shutterstock.com; p. 11 https://commons.wikimedia.org/wiki/File:Moschus_moschiferus_in_Plzen_zoo_(12.02.2011).jpg; p. 12 belizar/Shutterstock.com; p. 13 Rosa Jay/Shutterstock.com; p. 14 Heidi & Hans-Juergen Koch/Minden Pictures/Getty Images; p. 15 Kazakov Maksim/Shutterstock.com; p. 16 Mark Newman/Lonely Planet Images/Getty Images; p. 17 JIM ZIPP/Science Source/Shutterstock.com; p. 18 Seaphotoart/Shutterstock.com; p. 19 Kristel Segeren/Shutterstock.com; p. 20 enciktat/Shutterstock.com; p. 21 Stuart G Porter/Shutterstock.com; p. 22 Teguh Tirtaputra/Shutterstock.com.

Cataloging-in-Publication Data

Names: Cargill-Greer, Stephanie.
Title: Fighting with fangs and claws / Stephanie Cargill-Greer.
Description: New York : PowerKids Press, 2018. | Series: How animals adapt to survive | Includes index.
Identifiers: ISBN 9781538328385 (pbk.) | ISBN 9781508164357 (library bound) | ISBN 9781538328446 (6 pack)
Subjects: LCSH: Teeth–Juvenile literature. | Fangs–Juvenile literature. | Claws–Juvenile literature.
Classification: LCC QL858.C37 2018 | DDC 591.47–dc23

Manufactured in China

CPSIA Compliance Information: Batch #BW18PK: For Further Information contact Rosen Publishing, New York, New York at 1-800-237-9932

CONTENTS

SHARP ADAPTATIONS

All **environments** present challenges, and **adaptations** help animals survive in them. While some adaptations help animals hide or fly, the sharpest adaptations are fangs and claws. These adaptations are found in small spiders, large cats, and other, more surprising, creatures.

Fangs are long, sharp teeth. They are used to bite, hold, and tear the flesh of an animal's **prey**. Many animal **species** use fangs to deliver **venom** to prey and enemies.

Claws are pointed, curved nails made of **keratin**. Animal claws can be used for attacking and protection but also for holding on to things, digging, and climbing.

THE WORLD'S LONGEST

GABOON VIPER

LONGEST SNAKE FANG
up to 2 inches (5.08 cm)

CLOUDED LEOPARD

LONGEST BIG CAT FANG
(relative to size)
up to 2 inches (5.08 cm)

GIANT ARMADILLO

LONGEST MAMMAL CLAW
(relative to size)
up to 7.8 inches (20 cm)

THERIZINOSAURUS

LONGEST DINOSAUR CLAW
up to 3.2 feet (1 m)

SLITHER and STRIKE

Many people are afraid of snakes. In fact, it is one of the most common fears. People may fear snakes because of their fangs and the venom they may have. A venomous snake's fangs are hollow. This allows the fangs to **inject** venom into prey.

Adaptation Answers

One of the world's most venomous snakes is the Belcher's sea snake. One drop of this snake's venom could kill thousands of people. However, the Belcher's sea snake doesn't inject venom with every bite.

The venomous Great Lakes bush viper is a solenoglyphous snake, which means it has fangs that fold up into its jaw. Its fangs come down when it's ready to strike.

Fangs are usually found in the front of an animal's mouth. This helps it make quick attacks. Some venomous snakes—such as rattlesnakes, cobras, and vipers—have fangs in the front of their mouth. However, some venomous snakes are opisthoglyphous, or rear fanged. Rear-fanged snakes' fangs are curved backward and are found in the back of the upper jaw. This helps them hold on to prey to inject it with venom.

SMALL FANGS, BIG BITE

More than 40,000 species of spiders live on Earth, and new species are discovered all the time. Spiders may be small, but all of them have fangs and many of them are venomous. These fangs can be folded away when the spider doesn't need them.

Fangs and venom help spiders eat. Spiders have many ways to catch their prey, including webs. Once a spider has caught its prey, the spider uses its fangs to inject that prey with venom. This makes the prey unable to move and may kill it. It's easier for the spider to eat because its prey won't be able to escape.

Adaptation Answers

One of the most well-known spiders is the black widow. Its venom can cause severe pain and, on rare occasions, may kill humans. Thankfully, the female black widow is easy to recognize. She has a black body with a red hourglass on it.

The red hourglass shape on the female black widow spider's body warns other animals of her deadly bite.

HOW UNUSUAL: FANGED DEER

The last thing you might expect to see is a deer with fangs. However, the musk deer proves expectations wrong. Musk deer are small, but their short, sturdy bodies are perfect for climbing the mountains where they live in Asia.

Adaptation Answers

The musk deer's name comes from a **secretion** called musk, which comes from the deer's scent **gland**. Musk is popular in perfumes and old-fashioned medicines.

The males of most deer species grow antlers, or horns. Male musk deer don't grow antlers. Instead, they have long teeth that grow out of their mouth. Musk deer use their fangs to fight other males for **mates**. Male musk deer are very territorial. They only allow female deer to enter their **range**. If another male enters their range, they may fight.

Musk deer are shy. They hide during the day and come out to feed at night.

HANGING OUT with BATS

Bats are the only flying **mammals**, and they have many surprising adaptations. While bats are known for roosting, or sleeping, in caves, they also roost in trees, hollows, and sometimes buildings. Most bats are nocturnal, or active mainly at night.

Adaptation Answers

Vampire bats drink the blood of animals such as cows, pigs, and horses. They use their sharp fangs to cut their prey's skin. Then they lick the blood with their tongue.

The Egyptian fruit bat uses its claws to hold on to cave walls.

Bats have adapted to sleeping upside down for easy takeoff. Their clawed toes also help them hold on to uneven surfaces. Bats that hibernate, or spend the winter sleeping or resting, spend that time holding on to their roosting spot. They also have a claw on their thumbs, which are part of each wing. They use these claws to climb, hold on to food, and fight.

The CROAK and CLAW

The African clawed frog is the largest species of frog that has claws. Attached to each powerful back leg are five long toes. The middle three toes are clawed. These clawed toes are used to tear food into pieces. The African clawed frog has no tongue. It uses its front toes to push food into its mouth.

African clawed frogs are aquatic, which means they live most of their life in the water. They eat insects, small fish, and other creatures. African clawed frogs can survive on land for very short periods of time. They can't hop, but they can crawl on the ground.

The African clawed frog has clawed and **webbed** back toes but its front toes aren't webbed and don't have claws.

PREDATORS of the SKY

Peregrine falcons are fast, graceful birds. They belong to a group of hunting birds called raptors. Raptors are the only hunting birds that use their feet to catch prey. Peregrine falcons have strong, sharp, and slightly curved claws called talons, which they use to catch their prey midair.

A peregrine falcon's diet is 77 to 99 percent other birds. They also eat small animals such as bats, voles, and lemmings.

Peregrine falcons can reach speeds up to 200 miles (321.9 km) per hour when diving from the sky to catch their prey. However, they don't use their talons just to catch prey. They also use them to fight and carry prey. Falcons sometimes curl their talons into a fist to knock prey out of the air.

SLOW and STEADY

Sloths are mammals that live in trees in Central and South America. They're the world's slowest-moving mammals. Sloths have claws that range from 3 to 4 inches (7.6 to 10.2 cm) long. Sloths spend most of their time in trees. They have a hard time walking on the ground because their claws are so long.

Adaptation Answers

Sloths don't digest, or break down, food very fast due to the leaves they eat and their four-part stomachs. They may also be so slow because these leaves aren't very nutritious and they don't get much energy from eating them.

Sloths' claws are perfect for tree life. Sloths do almost everything in trees. They give birth, sleep, and eat there.

Sloths use their claws to climb and to help keep them safe from predators. They can use their claws and teeth with surprising speed if they're attacked. However, sloths' slow movements don't draw much attention from predators, which also helps keep them safe.

FEARSOME TIGERS

The cat family has some of the most skilled hunters in the animal kingdom. One of the fiercest predators in this family is the tiger. A tiger's mouth contains sharp teeth, including a set of fangs on the top and bottom jaws for biting into prey.

Cheetahs' claws are only semi-retractable. Their claws help keep them from slipping when they run.

Most cat claws can retract into, or go inside, their paws. This helps tigers stay silent while hunting prey. The claws appear when it is time to strike. Cats also have dewclaws. These are claws on the inside of each front foot. Dewclaws are used to hold on to prey and help cats climb.

FANGED FISH and CLAWED CRITTERS

Earth's oceans are also home to many animals with fangs. That includes anglerfish and a tiny fish called the fangblenny. Sea creatures with claws include crabs, lobsters, and otters. No matter where you go, you are sure to find animals with fangs and claws.

Adaptations help animals survive. Fangs and claws might sound scary to humans, but they are necessary adaptations for certain animals. They help animals hunt, eat, and protect themselves from predators.

PORCELAIN CRAB

GLOSSARY

adaptation: A change in a living thing that helps it live better in its environment.

environment: The conditions that surround a living thing and affect the way it lives.

gland: A body part that produces something that helps with a bodily function.

inject: To force something into the body using a needle or sharp teeth.

keratin: A kind of matter that makes up human hair and nails and other animal parts such as horns, feathers, and claws.

mammal: Any warm-blooded animal whose babies drink milk and whose body is covered with hair or fur.

mate: One of two animals that come together to make babies.

prey: An animal hunted by other animals for food.

range: The area of land over which animals move and feed.

secretion: Matter produced and given off by a plant or animal part.

species: A group of plants or animals that are all the same kind.

venom: A type of poison some animals make in their body and pass on to prey and enemies through fangs.

webbed: Having skin between the toes, as ducks, frogs, and some other animals that swim do.

INDEX

WEBSITES

Due to the changing nature of Internet links, PowerKids Press has developed an online list of websites related to the subject of this book. This site is updated regularly. Please use this link to access the list: www.powerkidslinks.com/haas/fang